frame > by > frame
baking

frame >by >frame
baking

the cookbook that shows you every step

LOVE FOOD

First published in 2009
Love Food ® is an imprint of Parragon Books Ltd

Parragon
Queen Street House
4 Queen Street
Bath BA1 1HE, UK

Love Food ® and the accompanying heart device is a trade mark of Parragon Books Ltd

ISBN: 978-1-4075-7803-3

Printed in China

Cover and internal design by Talking Design
Photography by Mike Cooper
Home economy by Lincoln Jefferson
Introduction and cover text by Linda Doeser
New recipes by Christine Last

Notes for the Reader

This book uses both metric and imperial measurements. Follow the same units of measurement throughout; do not mix metric and imperial. All spoon measurements are level: teaspoons are assumed to be 5 ml, and tablespoons are assumed to be 15 ml. Unless otherwise stated, milk is assumed to be full fat, eggs and individual vegetables are medium, and pepper is freshly ground black pepper.

The times given are an approximate guide only. Preparation times differ according to the techniques used by different people and the cooking times may also vary from those given. Optional ingredients, variations or serving suggestions have not been included in the calculations.

Recipes using raw or very lightly cooked eggs should be avoided by infants, the elderly, pregnant women, convalescents and anyone suffering from an illness. Pregnant and breastfeeding women are advised to avoid eating peanuts and peanut products. Sufferers from nut allergies should be aware that some of the ready-made ingredients used in the recipes in this book may contain nuts. Always check the packaging before use.

contents

introduction

This magnificent cookbook with its profusion of beautiful and immensely useful photographs will prove to be an invaluable addition to any cook's bookshelf. The recipes are clear, easy to follow, beautifully illustrated and simply scrumptious, so whatever your level of expertise in the kitchen you are virtually guaranteed success every time.

Every recipe starts with a photograph of all the ingredients but this is more than just a pretty picture or – even less helpful – a montage that is not to scale so that a pear appears to be the same size as an egg. Instead, it serves as a handy way of checking that you have everything ready before you start cooking. Just comparing the picture with the ingredients arranged on your own worktop or kitchen table will ensure that you haven't missed anything out and when it's time to add the glacé cherries, for example, you have already quartered them as specified in the ingredients list. If you're uncertain about how thinly to slice fruit or how dark to toast nuts, a glance at the photograph will provide an instant answer.

Each short and straightforward step of the method is clearly explained without any jargon or difficult technical terms. Once again, what you see in the photograph is what you should expect to see in front of you. Not only is this reassuring for the novice cook, but also those with more experience will find it a helpful reminder of the little touches that can easily be overlooked. Each recipe ends with a mouth-watering photograph of the finished cake, biscuits, tart or loaf.

Why you need this book

Even some quite experienced cooks find 'baking' a daunting prospect and think it's sure to be difficult. Yet, the word baking encompasses many different kinds of products from biscuits to bread and a variety of different techniques from creamed sponge cakes to choux pastry. They can't all be impossibly difficult and demanding and, in fact, most are astonishingly easy.

In this book there are over 50 easy-to-follow recipes for cakes, traybakes, sweet and savoury pastries, biscuits and bread – some traditional family favourites and others with a contemporary twist, some for special occasions and others for everyday treats. All of them are straightforward and, by using the unique frame by frame guide, even the novice cook will find they're figuratively and literally a piece of cake.

top tips for easy baking

* Read all the way through the recipe – ingredients list and method – before you start so that you know exactly what you will need. Scrabbling about at the back of the storecupboard to find a rarely used ingredient or moving half a dozen other utensils to reach the one you need in the middle of preparing a cake batter or bread dough is, at best, exasperating and, at worst, liable to spoil it.

* Apart from when you are making pastry dough by the rubbing-in method, collect all your ingredients together, including anything that is normally stored in the refrigerator, at least half an hour before you start cooking to bring them to room temperature. Eggs are particularly important because if they are too cold when they are added, they tend to curdle. Remove mixing bowls from the cupboard to bring them to room temperature too.

* When making pastry dough, collect the dry ingredients and any filling ingredients together ready for use and put a jug of water in the refrigerator to chill. (Keeping the dough cold is essential for crisp results.)

* Accurate measurement of the ingredients is more important for baking than for any other kind of cooking. Weigh dry ingredients on reliable kitchen scales and measure liquids in a measuring jug or, for small quantities, standard measuring spoons. Use medium eggs unless another size is specified in the recipe.

* Always preheat the oven to the specified temperature. An oven that is not hot enough will cause baked goods to sink, while one that is too hot can cause them to crack. If you're unsure about the reliability of your thermostat, invest in an oven thermometer and use that to check the temperature.

* The type of flour used for baking is important and substituting one for another may produce disappointing results. Plain flour is used for pastry dough and anything that does not need a raising agent. Self-raising flour has added baking powder and is used for many different kinds of cakes. Strong bread flour has a high gluten content that produces an elastic dough when kneaded. Wholemeal flour is made from the whole grain and produces a denser, nuttier, slightly more chewy texture than white flour. If you do want to use it – in pastry dough, for example, substitute it for only half the quantity of white flour in the recipe. Whatever flour you are using, it is always worth sifting it to add air and remove any lumps, even if it is described as ready-sifted on the packet.

* Bread recipes often require yeast and may specify using hand-hot liquid. Yeast works best at a temperature of 21–36°C/70–97°F. Do not use hotter water as this will kill the yeast and prevent it from producing the gases that cause the bread to rise.

* Always use the size and shape of baking tin specified in the recipe. A tin that is too large will result in cracks and airholes and one that is too small is likely to cause the cake or loaf to burn.

* Follow the recipe instructions for cooling. Some cakes and biscuits are fragile and should be left for a short while in the tin to firm up slightly before turning out onto a wire cooling rack. Others should be turned out onto the rack immediately after they have been removed from the oven or the base will become soggy. Heavy cakes are usually allowed to cool completely in the tin.

time-saving shortcuts

✳ Melt chocolate in the microwave oven. Break it into pieces and put it into a microwave-proof bowl. Heat on MEDIUM for 10 seconds, then stir. Return to the oven and heat for another 10 seconds before checking and stirring again – even when it's melted it will hold its shape so you cannot tell if it's ready just by looking at it. White chocolate should be heated on LOW.

✳ Toast nuts in the microwave to avoid burning. Spread out 4 tablespoons nuts on a microwave-proof plate and cook on HIGH for 5 minutes.

✳ All is not lost if you have forgotten to remove the butter from the refrigerator in advance – just microwave on HIGH for 15–20 seconds.

✳ The easiest way to peel fruits such as nectarines and peaches, as well as tomatoes, is to slit their skins, put them into a heatproof bowl and pour in boiling water to cover. Leave to stand for 30–60 seconds and drain. The skins will slip off much more easily.

✳ When measuring small quantities of something sticky such as honey or syrup, stand the spoon in hot water for a minute. It will then drop off the spoon easily.

✳ If dough is sticky, even after chilling in the refrigerator, roll it out between sheets of baking parchment or clingfilm. You can use the bottom sheet to help you transfer it to the baking sheet.

useful equipment

* **Kitchen scales:** It is important to be precise when weighing ingredients for baking. Electronic scales are the most accurate but the batteries do need replacing quite frequently. Spring scales are very easy to use, while old-fashioned balance scales are accurate but a little more fiddly.

* **Measuring jugs:** These are available in a variety of shapes and sizes. It is easier to measure liquids accurately using a tall, thin jug than a short fat one and a clear jug is more useful than an opaque one.

* **Measuring spoons:** Ordinary spoons vary in size so you will need at least one set of standard measuring spoons. As they are inexpensive, it's worth buying several sets so that you don't have to keep washing them throughout the recipe.

* **Mixing bowls:** You will need a selection of different sizes – large for mixing dough and cake batters, medium for measuring out ingredients and small for melting chocolate, mixing icing, etc. Both heatproof glass and ceramic bowls are useful; remember that metal bowls cannot be used in the microwave.

* **Sieves:** A strong fine wire sieve is essential for sifting dry ingredients to aerate them. A small sieve is useful for dusting cakes and biscuits with icing sugar.

* **Spoons and spatulas:** A set of wooden spoons in different sizes is invaluable for all kinds of tasks from stirring a melted chocolate mixture in a hot pan to pressing fruit through a sieve. A long-handled metal spoon is perfect for folding dry ingredients into a whisked mixture. Flexible rubber or plastic spatulas, available in a variety of sizes, are useful for stirring, mixing, folding and scraping all the cake batter out of the bowl.

* **Pastry blender:** This tool is used for working fat into flour rather than using your fingertips. It helps to keep the mixture cool but is not essential.

* **Whisks:** A hand-held balloon whisk is useful for many tasks from aerating egg whites to whisking cream. A hand-held electric whisk takes the hard work out of these processes, is strong enough to cream butter and sugar mixtures and can be used in a hot pan.

* **Rolling pin:** These can be made of wood, glass, marble or plastic and some can be filled with cold water to keep dough cool. Choose a heavy rolling pin that will do the job without you having to press down and so distort the dough.

* **Pastry board:** Marble is the best surface because it keeps the dough cool and requires only a very light dusting of flour. Wood is popular and, as it's a poor conductor of heat, it's also good for rolling out pastry and biscuit doughs.

* **Biscuit and pastry cutters:** These are available in a wide range of sizes and shapes with plain or fluted edges. Metal cutters produce a cleaner edge than plastic ones.

* **Cake tins:** Heavy gauge cake tins distribute the heat evenly and prevent scorching. It is a matter of personal choice whether you prefer them with a non-stick lining. Round tins are used more often than other shapes, but always check the recipe. The most useful sizes are shallow 20-cm/8-inch sandwich tins for sponge cakes and deep 23–25-cm/9–10-inch tins for larger cakes. A Swiss roll tin is rectangular and very shallow, while a slightly deeper rectangular tin may be used for traybakes Other specialist tins include springform tins, which have a clip on the side, making it easy to remove the tin from very fragile cakes, and angel cake tins with a central tube projecting above the rim.

* **Loaf tins:** Bread is quite often baked on a flat baking sheet as the dough is dense enough to retain its shape. When a tin is used, the base and sides of the loaf are contained, so the dough expands upwards, creating a denser crumb and crisp crust. Loaf tins are usually rectangular and popular sizes are 17 x 11 x 8 cm/6½ x 4¼ x 3¼ inches and 19 x 12 x 9 cm/7½ x 4½ x 3½ inches. They are available with non-stick linings.

* **Bun, muffin and tart tins:** Available with a non-stick coating if you prefer, bun tins are perfect for small cakes and individual sweet or savoury tarts. A 12-cup tray is a useful size. Muffin trays have deep cups with flared sides that encourage the dough to rise. Large tarts can be made in ovenproof glass or ceramic dishes, but metal ones distribute the heat more quickly and evenly. They are usually round and may be plain or fluted and with or without a removable base. They are available in a range of sizes; deeper tins are best for tarts that require a firm crust to support a cream- or egg-based filling, while shallower tins are ideal for glazed fruit tarts.

* **Baking sheets and trays:** It is best to buy heavy sheets and trays as they do not buckle or wobble and distribute the heat evenly. Baking sheets usually have a slightly sloping edge to make it easier to lift them and are used for many kinds of loaves, pastries and some types of biscuits. Baking trays have a rim around the entire edge to prevent runny doughs from falling off.

* **Cooling rack:** Wire racks are made in a wide variety of shapes and sizes. They let air circulate around a cake or biscuits, preventing trapped moisture from making them soggy while they cool.

small cakes & biscuits

fairy cupcakes

makes 16 cupcakes

ingredients
115 g/4 oz unsalted butter
115 g/4 oz caster sugar
2 eggs, beaten
115 g/4 oz self-raising flour
sugar flowers, hundreds and
   thousands, glacé cherries
   and/or chocolate strands, to
   decorate

icing
200 g/7 oz icing sugar
about 2 tbsp lukewarm water
few drops of food colouring
   (optional)

>1 Preheat the oven to 180°C/350°F/Gas Mark 4.
Put 16 double-layer paper cases on a baking
sheet.

>2 Place the butter and caster sugar in
a large bowl and cream together
until pale and fluffy. Gradually add
the eggs, beating well after each
addition. Fold in the flour, using a
metal spoon.

Decorate the cupcakes with sugar flowers, hundreds and thousands and glacé cherries, and serve.

>3 Spoon the mixture into the paper cases and bake in the preheated oven for 15–20 minutes, until well risen. Remove from the oven and place on a wire rack to cool.

>4 For the icing, sift the icing sugar into a bowl and add enough water to mix to a smooth paste, thick enough to coat the back of a spoon. Stir in a few drops of food colouring, if using, then spread over the cakes.

chocolate butterfly cupcakes

makes 12 cupcakes

ingredients

125 g/4½ oz margarine,
  softened
125 g/4½ oz caster sugar
150 g/5½ oz self-raising flour,
  sifted

2 large eggs
2 tbsp cocoa powder
25 g/1 oz plain chocolate,
  melted

lemon buttercream
100 g/3½ oz unsalted butter,
  softened
225 g/8 oz icing sugar, sifted,
  plus extra for dusting

grated rind of ½ lemon
1 tbsp lemon juice

>1 Preheat the oven to 180°C/350°F/Gas Mark 4. Place 12 paper cases in a shallow bun tin.

>2 Place the margarine, caster sugar, flour, eggs and cocoa powder in a large bowl, and beat until the mixture is just smooth. Beat in the melted chocolate.

>3 Spoon the mixture into the paper cases, filling them three-quarters full.

>4 Bake in the preheated oven for 15 minutes, or until well risen. Remove from the oven and place on a wire rack to cool.

For the buttercream, place the butter in a mixing bowl and beat until fluffy. Gradually add in the icing sugar, lemon rind and lemon juice, beating well with each addition.

Cut the top off each cake, using a serrated knife. Cut each cake top in half. Spread the lemon buttercream over the cut surface of each cake and push the two pieces of cake top into the icing to form wings.

Dust with icing sugar and serve.

low-fat blueberry muffins

makes 12 muffins

ingredients

225 g/8 oz plain flour
1 tsp bicarbonate of soda
¼ tsp salt

1 tsp ground allspice
115 g/4 oz caster sugar
3 large egg whites
3 tbsp low-fat margarine

150 ml/5 fl oz thick low-fat
natural yogurt or blueberry-
flavoured yogurt

1 tsp vanilla extract
85 g/3 oz fresh blueberries

>1 Preheat the oven to 190°C/375°F/Gas Mark 5. Place 12 paper cases in a shallow bun tin.

>2 Sift the flour, bicarbonate of soda, salt and half the allspice into a large mixing bowl. Add six tablespoons of the sugar and mix together well.

>3 In a separate bowl, whisk the egg whites together. Add the margarine, yogurt and vanilla extract and mix together well, then stir in the blueberries until thoroughly mixed.

>4 Add the fruit mixture to the dry ingredients, then gently stir until just combined. Do not overstir – it is fine for it to be a little lumpy.

23

> **5** Divide the mixture evenly between the paper cases to about two-thirds full. Mix the remaining sugar with the remaining allspice and sprinkle over the muffins.

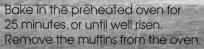

> **6** Bake in the preheated oven for 25 minutes, or until well risen. Remove the muffins from the oven.

Leave to cool or serve warm.

lemon poppy seed madeleines

makes about 30 madeleines

ingredients
oil, for greasing
3 eggs
1 egg yolk
finely grated rind of
 1 lemon
140 g/5 oz golden caster
 sugar
140 g/5 oz plain flour
1 tsp baking powder
140 g/5 oz unsalted
 butter, melted and
 cooled
1 tbsp poppy seeds

>1 Preheat the oven to 190°C/375°F/Gas Mark 5.
Lightly grease three 12-hole madeleine tins.

>2 Whisk the eggs, yolk, lemon rind and
sugar in a large bowl until very pale
and thick.

Turn out the cakes and cool on a wire rack, then serve very fresh.

>3 Sift the flour and baking powder over the mix and fold in lightly using a metal spoon. Fold in the melted butter and poppy seeds.

>4 Spoon into the tins and bake in the preheated oven for about 10 minutes, until well risen.

double ginger cupcakes

makes about 12 cupcakes

ingredients
175 g/6 oz plain flour
1 tbsp baking powder
2 tsp ground ginger
175 g/6 oz unsalted butter,
  softened

175 g/6 oz light muscovado
  sugar
3 eggs, beaten
25 g/1 oz crystallized stem
  ginger, finely chopped

frosting
200 g/7 oz ricotta cheese
85 g/3 oz icing sugar, sifted
finely grated rind 1 tangerine
diced crystallized ginger,
  to decorate

> **1** Preheat the oven to 190°C/375°F/Gas Mark 5. Place 12 paper cases in a shallow bun tin.

> **2** Sift the flour, baking powder and ground ginger into a large bowl.

> **3** Add the butter, muscovado sugar and eggs and beat well until smooth. Stir in the crystallized ginger.

> **4** Spoon the mixture into the paper cases. Bake in the preheated oven for 15–20 minutes, until well risen. Remove from the oven and place on a wire rack to cool.

>**6** Spoon a little frosting onto each cake and spread over the surface to cover.

Top the cupcakes with diced crystallized ginger and serve.

frosted peanut butter cupcakes

makes 16 cupcakes

ingredients

55 g/2 oz butter, softened
225 g/8 oz soft light brown sugar
115 g/4 oz crunchy peanut butter

2 eggs, lightly beaten
1 tsp vanilla extract
225 g/8 oz plain white flour
2 tsp baking powder
100 ml/3½ fl oz milk

frosting

200 g/7 oz cream cheese
25 g/1 oz butter, softened
225 g/8 oz icing sugar

> 1 Preheat the oven to 180°C/350°F/Gas Mark 4. Put 16 double-layer paper cases on a baking sheet.

> 2 Put the butter, sugar and peanut butter in a bowl and beat together until well mixed. Gradually add the eggs, beating well after each addition, then add the vanilla extract.

> 3 Sift in the flour and baking powder, then use a metal spoon to fold in, alternating with the milk.

> 4 Spoon the mixture into the paper cases and bake in the preheated oven for 25 minutes, or until well risen and golden brown. Remove from the oven and place on a wire rack to cool.

>5 For the frosting, put the cream cheese and butter into a large bowl and beat together until smooth. Sift in the icing sugar, then beat until well mixed.

>6 When the cupcakes are cold, spread some frosting on top of each, swirling with a round-bladed knife.

Store in the refrigerator until ready to serve.

chocolate chip cookies

makes 8 cookies

ingredients

unsalted butter, melted,
 for greasing
175 g/6 oz plain flour, sifted
1 tsp baking powder
125 g/4½ oz margarine, melted
85 g/3 oz light muscovado
 sugar
55 g/2 oz caster sugar
½ tsp vanilla extract
1 egg
125 g/4½ oz plain chocolate
 chips

 1 Preheat the oven to 190°C/375°F/Gas Mark 5. Line and lightly grease two baking trays.

2 Place all of the ingredients in a large mixing bowl and beat until well combined.

Serve or store in an
airtight box.

> **3** Place well-spaced tablespoonfuls of the
mixture onto the prepared baking trays.

> **4** Bake in the preheated oven for 10–12 minutes,
or until golden brown. Remove from the oven
and place on a wire rack to cool.

frosted cherry rings

makes 15–18 rings

ingredients

115 g/4 oz unsalted butter, plus extra for greasing
85 g/3 oz golden caster sugar

1 egg yolk
finely grated rind of ½ lemon
200 g/7 oz plain flour, plus extra for dusting

55 g/2 oz glacé cherries, finely chopped

icing

85 g/3 oz icing sugar, sifted
1½ tbsp lemon juice

>1 Preheat the oven to 200°C/400°F/Gas Mark 6. Lightly grease two baking trays.

>2 Cream together the butter and caster sugar until pale and fluffy. Beat in the egg yolk and lemon rind.

>3 Sift in the flour, stir, then add the glacé cherries, mixing with your hands to a soft dough.

>4 Roll out the dough on a lightly floured surface to about 5 mm/¼ inch thick. Stamp out 8-cm/3¼-inch rounds with a biscuit cutter.

>5 Stamp out the centre of each round with a 2.5-cm/1-inch cutter and place the rings on the prepared baking trays. Re-roll any trimmings and cut more biscuits.

 >6 Bake in the preheated oven for 12–15 minutes, until firm and golden brown.

 >7 Allow to cool on the baking trays for 2 minutes, then transfer to a wire rack to finish cooling.

 >8 For the frosting, mix the icing sugar to a smooth paste with the lemon juice. Drizzle over the biscuits and leave until set.

Serve with tea or coffee as a
mid-morning treat.

mini florentines

makes 20–30 florentines

ingredients
75 g/2¾ oz butter
75 g/2¾ oz caster sugar
25 g/1 oz sultanas or raisins
25 g/1 oz glacé cherries, chopped
25 g/1 oz crystallized stem ginger, finely chopped
25 g/1 oz sunflower seeds
100 g/3½ oz flaked almonds
2 tbsp double cream
175 g/6 oz plain or milk chocolate, broken into pieces

>1 Preheat the oven to 180°C/350°F/ Gas Mark 4. Line two baking trays.

>2 Place the butter in a small saucepan and melt over a low heat. Add the sugar, stir until dissolved, then bring to the boil.

>3 Remove from the heat and stir in the sultanas, glacé cherries, crystallized ginger, sunflower seeds and almonds. Mix well, then beat in the cream.

>4 Place small, well-spaced teaspoons of mixture onto the prepared baking trays. Bake in the preheated oven for 10–12 minutes, or until light golden in colour.

>5 Remove from the oven and, while still hot, use a circular biscuit cutter to pull in the edges to form perfect circles. Leave to cool and turn crisp before removing from the baking trays.

>6 Put the chocolate in a heatproof bowl set over a saucepan of gently simmering water and stir until melted. Spread most of the chocolate onto a sheet of baking paper.

>7 When the chocolate is on the point of setting, place the biscuits flat-side down on the chocolate and let it harden completely.

>8 Cut around the florentines and remove from the baking paper. Spread the remaining chocolate on the coated side of the florentines, using a fork to mark waves. Leave to set.

Serve or present as a gift in a pretty box.

classic oatmeal biscuits

makes 10–12 biscuits

ingredients

175 g/6 oz butter or
  margarine, plus extra for
  greasing
275 g/9¾ oz demerara
  sugar
1 egg
4 tbsp water
1 tsp vanilla extract
375 g/13 oz rolled oats
140 g/5 oz plain flour, sifted
1 tsp salt
½ tsp bicarbonate of soda

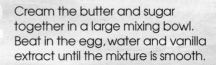

> **1** Preheat the oven to 350°F/180°C/Gas Mark 4
> and grease a large baking sheet.

> **2** Cream the butter and sugar
> together in a large mixing bowl.
> Beat in the egg, water and vanilla
> extract until the mixture is smooth.

For a sweeter option, drizzle with melted chocolate.

>3 In a separate bowl, mix the oats, flour, salt and bicarbonate of soda. Gradually stir the oat mixture into the creamed mixture until thoroughly combined.

>4 Place small, well-spaced teaspoons of mixture onto the prepared baking tray. Bake in the preheated oven for 15 minutes, or until golden brown. Remove from the oven and place on a wire rack to cool.

polenta berry crunch buns

makes 18 buns

ingredients

225 g/8 oz self-raising flour,
  sifted
85 g/3 oz polenta
150 g/5½ oz golden caster
  sugar

150 g/5½ oz unsalted butter
finely grated rind of 1 lemon
1 egg, beaten
2–3 tbsp lemon juice
150 g/5½ oz mixed berries

> **1** Preheat the oven to 200°C/400°F/Gas Mark 6. Place 18 paper cases in 2 shallow bun tins.

> **2** Place the flour, polenta, sugar and butter in a food processor and process to resemble fine breadcrumbs.

> **3** Stir the lemon rind into the mixture.

> **4** Stir in the egg with just enough lemon juice to make a soft, crumbly dough.

>5 Fold in the berries with a metal spoon, mixing evenly.

>6 Spoon the mixture into the paper cases and bake for about 20 minutes, until golden brown. Cool the cakes on a wire rack.

The cakes can be stored for 2–3 days in an airtight container, or frozen for up to 1 month.

cranberry & pine nut biscotti

makes 18–20 biscotti

ingredients

butter or oil, for greasing
85 g/3 oz light muscovado
  sugar

1 large egg
140 g/5 oz plain flour
½ tsp baking powder
1 tsp ground allspice

55 g/2 oz dried cranberries
55 g/2 oz pine nuts, toasted

1 Preheat the oven to 180°C/350°F/Gas Mark 4. Grease a baking sheet.

>2 Whisk together the sugar and egg until pale and thick enough to form a trail.

>3 Sift the flour, baking powder and allspice and fold into the mixture.

>4 Stir in the cranberries and pine nuts and mix lightly to a smooth dough.

> **5** With lightly floured hands, shape the mixture into a long roll, about 28 cm/ 11 inch long. Press to flatten slightly.

> **6** Lift the dough onto the baking sheet and bake in the preheated oven for 20–25 minutes, until golden.

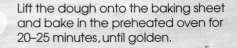

> **7** Cool for 3–4 minutes, then cut into 1.5-cm/ ⅝-inch thick slices and arrange on the baking sheet.

> **8** Bake in the preheated oven for 10 minutes, or until golden. Remove from the oven and place on a wire rack to cool.

When cool, enjoy fresh or
store the biscotti in an airtight
container for 2–3 weeks.

chocolate hazelnut flapjack cookies

makes 16–18 cookies

ingredients
85 g/3 oz unsalted butter,
  plus extra for greasing
175 g/6 oz chocolate
  hazelnut spread
175 g/6 oz porridge oats
70 g/2½ oz blanched
  hazelnuts, chopped

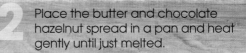

> **1** Preheat the oven to 200°C/400°F/Gas Mark 6.
> Grease a baking sheet.

> **2** Place the butter and chocolate
> hazelnut spread in a pan and heat
> gently until just melted.

The cookies can be stored in an airtight container for up to 2 weeks.

>3 Add the porridge oats and hazelnuts to the chocolate mixture and stir to combine thoroughly.

>4 Shape the mixture into 16–18 equal-size balls, then press onto the prepared baking sheet. Bake in the preheated oven for 10–12 minutes, remove from the oven and leave until firm before transferring the cookies to a wire rack to finish cooling.

cakes & traybakes

victoria sponge cake

serves 8

ingredients
175 g/6 oz butter, softened,
  plus extra for greasing
175 g/6 oz self-raising flour
1 tsp baking powder
175 g/6 oz golden caster sugar
3 eggs
icing sugar, sifted, for dusting

filling
3 tbsp raspberry jam
300 ml/10 fl oz double cream,
  whipped
16 fresh strawberries, halved

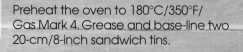

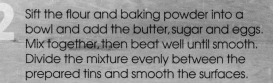

> **>1** Preheat the oven to 180°C/350°F/
> Gas Mark 4. Grease and base-line two
> 20-cm/8-inch sandwich tins.

> **>2** Sift the flour and baking powder into a
> bowl and add the butter, sugar and eggs.
> Mix together, then beat well until smooth.
> Divide the mixture evenly between the
> prepared tins and smooth the surfaces.

Dust with icing sugar and serve.

> **3** Bake in the preheated oven for 25–30 minutes, or until well risen and golden brown. Cool in the tins for 5 minutes, then turn out onto a wire rack to cool completely.

> **4** Sandwich together with jam, cream and strawberry halves.

chocolate fudge cake

serves 8

ingredients

175 g/6 oz unsalted butter, softened, plus extra for greasing
175 g/6 oz golden caster sugar
3 eggs, beaten
3 tbsp golden syrup
40 g/1½ oz ground almonds
175 g/6 oz self-raising flour
pinch of salt
40 g/1½ oz cocoa powder

icing

225 g/8 oz plain chocolate, broken into pieces
55 g/2 oz dark muscovado sugar
225 g/8 oz unsalted butter, diced
5 tbsp evaporated milk
½ tsp vanilla extract

>1 Preheat the oven to 180°C/350°F/Gas Mark 4. Grease and line two 20-cm/8-inch sandwich tins.

>2 For the icing, place the ingredients in a heavy-based saucepan. Heat gently, stirring constantly, until melted.

>3 Pour into a bowl and leave to cool. Cover and chill for 1 hour, or until spreadable.

>4 For the cake, place the butter and sugar in a bowl and beat together until light and fluffy. Gradually beat in the eggs. Stir in the golden syrup and almonds.

> **5** Sift the flour, salt and cocoa powder into a separate bowl, then fold into the mixture. Add a little water, if necessary, to make a dropping consistency.

> **6** Spoon the mixture into the prepared tins and bake in the preheated oven for 30–35 minutes, or until springy to the touch and a skewer inserted in the centre comes out clean.

> **7** Cool in the tins for 5 minutes, then turn out onto a wire rack to cool completely.

> **8** When the cakes are cold, sandwich them together with half the icing. Spread the remaining icing over the top and sides of the cake, swirling it to give a frosted appearance.

Cut into slices and serve.

rich almond cake

serves 8

ingredients

butter, for greasing
250 g/9 oz ricotta cheese
4 eggs, separated

1 tsp almond essence
175 g/6 oz golden caster sugar
250 g/9 oz ground almonds
finely grated rind of 1 lime

toasted flaked almonds,
 to decorate
icing sugar, sifted, for dusting

>1 Preheat the oven to 150°C/300°F/
Gas Mark 2. Grease and line a
23-cm/9-inch round cake tin.

>2 Beat together the ricotta, egg yolks, almond
essence and sugar. Stir in the almonds and
lime rind.

>3 Whisk the egg whites in a clean bowl until
they form soft peaks.

>4 Fold the whites lightly into the ricotta mixture,
using a large metal spoon.

>5 Spread the mixture into the tin and bake in the preheated oven for 50–60 minutes, until firm and lightly browned.

>6 Cool the cake in the tin for 10 minutes, then turn out onto a wire rack and sprinkle with flaked almonds.

Dust with icing sugar and serve.

coffee & walnut roulade

serves 6

ingredients

butter or oil, for greasing
3 eggs
1 egg white
115 g/4 oz golden caster sugar,
    plus extra for sprinkling

1 tsp coffee extract
75 g/2¾ oz plain flour, sifted
30 g finely chopped walnuts
roughly chopped walnuts,
    to decorate

filling

175 ml/6 fl oz double cream
40 g/1½ oz icing sugar, plus
    extra, sifted, for dusting
1 tbsp coffee liqueur

>1 Preheat the oven to 200°C/400°F/Gas Mark 6. Grease a 33 x 22 cm-/13 x 8½-inch Swiss roll tin and line with non-stick baking parchment.

>2 Place the eggs, egg white and sugar in a bowl over a pan of very hot water. Whisk with an electric whisk until pale and thick enough to leave a trail.

>3 Whisk in the coffee extract, then fold in the flour and walnuts lightly with a metal spoon.

>4 Spoon into the tin, spreading evenly. Bake in the preheated oven for 12–15 minutes, until golden brown and firm.

>5 Sprinkle a sheet of baking parchment with caster sugar. Turn out the roulade onto the paper and peel off the lining paper. Trim the edges.

>6 Quickly roll up the sponge from one short side, with the paper inside. Cool completely.

>7 For the filling, place the cream, sugar and liqueur in a bowl and whisk until the mixture begins to hold its shape.

>8 Carefully unroll the roulade, remove the paper and spread the cream over. Roll up carefully.

Dust with icing sugar and top with roughly chopped walnuts.

caramel peach gateau

serves 6–8

ingredients

175 g/6 oz unsalted butter, softened, plus extra for greasing
175 g/6 oz light muscovado sugar

3 eggs, beaten
1 tsp vanilla extract
175 g/6 oz self-raising flour
½ tsp baking powder
2 tbsp milk

filling

2 tbsp maple syrup
200 ml/7 fl oz thick crème fraîche (40% fat)
3 ripe peaches, thinly sliced

>1 Preheat the oven to 180°C/350°F/Gas Mark 4. Grease and base-line two 23-cm/9-inch round sandwich tins.

>2 Place the butter, sugar, eggs and vanilla extract in a bowl and sift over the flour and baking powder.

>3 Beat with an electric mixer until smooth, then add milk to make a soft consistency.

>4 Divide the mix between the tins and spread evenly.

>5 Bake in the preheated oven for 25–30 minutes, until firm and golden. Cool in the tins for 2 minutes, then turn out onto a wire rack to cool completely.

>6 Swirl 1 tbsp maple syrup into the crème fraîche and spread half over each cake.

>7 Arrange half the peach slices over one cake and top with the remaining cake, crème fraîche side down.

>8 Arrange the remaining peach slices over the top of the cake.

Brush the peach slices with maple syrup just before serving. Serve the cake on the day of filling.

apple streusel bars

makes 14 bars

ingredients

125 g/4½ oz unsalted
  butter, softened,
  plus extra
  for greasing
2 crisp eating
  apples, peeled,
  cored and diced
2 tbsp lemon juice
125 g/4½ oz golden
  caster sugar
1 tsp vanilla extract
2 eggs, beaten
150 g/5½ oz
  self-raising flour

topping

40 g/1½ oz blanched
  almonds, finely
  chopped
40 g/1½ oz plain flour
40 g/1½ oz light
  muscovado sugar
½ tsp ground
  cinnamon
30 g/1 oz unsalted
  butter, melted

> **1** Preheat the oven to 180°C/350°F/Gas Mark 4. Grease and line a 28 x 18-cm/11 x 7-inch traybake tin. Sprinkle the apples with lemon juice.

> **2** Cream together the butter, sugar and vanilla extract until pale. Gradually add the eggs, beating thoroughly.

Cut into bars and serve cold or warm.

>3 Sift over the flour and fold in evenly, then stir in the apples. Spread evenly in the tin.

>4 For the topping, mix all the ingredients to a crumbly texture, sprinkle over the cake and bake in the preheated oven for 45–55 minutes, unti firm and golden.

banana coconut loaf cake

makes 1 loaf

ingredients

90 ml/3 fl oz sunflower oil, plus
  extra for greasing
250 g/9 oz plain flour
1½ tsp baking powder

200 g/7 oz caster sugar
55 g/2 oz desiccated coconut
2 eggs
2 ripe bananas, mashed
125 ml/4 fl oz soured cream

1 tsp vanilla extract
long shred coconut, toasted,
  to decorate

Preheat the oven to 180°C/350°F/Gas Mark 4. Grease and line a 1-litre/1¾ pint loaf tin.

 Sift together the flour and baking powder in a large bowl.

 Stir in the sugar and coconut.

 Beat together the eggs, oil, bananas, cream and vanilla extract in a large bowl.

81

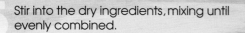

>5 Stir into the dry ingredients, mixing until evenly combined.

6 Spoon into the prepared tin, levelling with a palette knife.

>7 Bake in the preheated oven for about 1 hour or until risen, firm and golden brown.

8 Cool in the tin for 15 minutes, then turn out onto a wire rack to cool completely.

Decorate with shreds of coconut and serve.

blueberry & passionfruit drizzle squares

makes 9 squares

ingredients
150 g/5½ oz butter, softened, plus extra for greasing
2 eggs

175 g/6 oz golden caster sugar
175 g/6 oz self-raising flour, sifted
90 ml/3 fl oz milk

finely grated zest of 1 lemon
225 g/8 oz blueberries

syrup
4 ripe passionfruit
115 g/4 oz icing sugar, plus extra, sifted, for dusting

> **1** Preheat the oven to 190°C/375°F/Gas Mark 5. Grease and base-line a 23-cm/9-inch square cake tin.

> **2** Whisk the butter, eggs and sugar until pale and fluffy. Fold in the flour lightly and evenly.

> **3** Stir in the milk, lemon zest and 175 g/6 oz blueberries. Spread into the cake tin.

> **4** Bake in the preheated oven for 25–30 minutes, until firm and golden brown. Remove from the oven and leave in the tin.

>5 Meanwhile, make the syrup. Scoop the pulp from the passionfruit and rub through a sieve. Discard the pips.

>6 Place the sugar and passionfruit juice in a saucepan and heat gently, stirring, until the sugar dissolves.

>7 Prick the warm cake with a fork and spoon the syrup evenly over the surface.

>8 Leave the cake to cool completely in the tin then cut into 9 squares.

Top the squares with the reserved blueberries and dust with icing sugar before serving.

classic cherry cake

serves 8

ingredients

200 g/7 oz unsalted butter,
  plus extra for greasing
250 g/9 oz glacé cherries,
  quartered

85 g/3 oz ground almonds
200 g/7 oz plain flour
1 tsp baking powder
200 g/7 oz caster sugar
3 large eggs

finely grated rind and juice
  of 1 lemon
6 sugar cubes, crushed

>1
Preheat the oven to 180°C/350°F/ Gas Mark 4. Grease and line a 20-cm/8-inch round cake tin.

>2
Stir together the cherries, almonds and 1 tablespoon of the flour. Sift the remaining flour into a separate bowl with the baking powder.

>3
Cream together the butter and sugar until light and fluffy. Gradually add the eggs, beating hard, until evenly mixed.

>4
Add the flour mixture and fold lightly and evenly into the creamed mixture with a metal spoon. Add the cherry mixture, fold in evenly, then fold in the lemon rind and juice.

89

> **5** Spoon the mixture into the prepared tin and sprinkle with the crushed sugar cubes. Bake in the preheated oven for 1–1¼ hours, or until risen and golden brown and shrinking from the sides of the tin.

> **6** Leave to cool in the tin for about 15 minutes, then turn out onto a wire rack to cool completely.

Cut into slices and serve as
a mid-morning treat.

orange madeira ring

serves 8

ingredients

175 g/6 oz unsalted butter,
plus extra for greasing

1 tbsp golden syrup (plus extra
for drizzling, if liked)

2 medium oranges

175 g/6 oz caster sugar

3 eggs, beaten

115 g/4 oz plain flour

115 g/4 oz self-raising flour

finely grated rind of 1 orange

2–3 tbsp orange juice

> 1 Preheat the oven to 160°C/325°F/Gas Mark 3. Grease a 1.5-litre/2¾-pint ring cake tin and spoon the syrup into the base.

> 2 Cut all the white peel and pith from the oranges and slice.

> 3 Arrange the orange slices over the syrup in the tin.

> 4 Cream together the butter and sugar until pale and fluffy.

>5 Gradually beat in the eggs, beating well after each addition.

>6 Sift the flours into the mix and fold in, adding the orange rind and enough juice to make a soft batter.

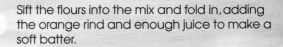

>7 Spoon the mixture into the tin and smooth the surface.

>8 Bake in the preheated oven for 45–55 minutes or until risen, golden and firm. Cool in the tin for 10 minutes, then turn out onto a wire rack to cool completely.

The cake can be served cold, or warm with extra golden syrup drizzled over.

95

chocolate chip brownies

makes 12 brownies

ingredients

225 g/8 oz butter, softened, plus
  extra for greasing
150 g/5½ oz plain chocolate,
  broken into pieces

225 g/8 oz self-raising flour
125 g/4½ oz caster sugar
4 eggs, beaten
75 g/2¾ oz pistachio nuts,
  chopped

100 g/3½ oz white chocolate,
  roughly chopped
icing sugar, sifted, for dusting

> **1** Preheat the oven to 180°C/350°F/Gas Mark 4. Grease and line a 23-cm/9-inch square baking tin.

> **2** Place the plain chocolate and the butter in a heatproof bowl set over a saucepan of simmering water. Stir until melted, then leave to cool slightly.

> **3** Sift the flour into a separate bowl and stir in the caster sugar.

> **4** Stir the eggs into the chocolate mixture, then pour into the flour and sugar and beat well.

>5 Stir in the nuts and white chocolate.

>6 Pour the mixture into the prepared tin, using a palette knife to spread evenly.

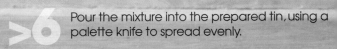

>7 Bake in the preheated oven for 30–35 minutes, or until firm to the touch around the edges. Cool in the tin for 20 minutes, then turn out onto a wire rack to cool completely.

>8 Dust with icing sugar and leave to cool completely.

Cut into 12 squares and serve.

double chocolate mint sponge

serves 8

ingredients

175 g/6 oz unsalted butter, softened, plus extra for greasing
150 g/5½ oz plain flour
2 tbsp cocoa powder
1 tbsp baking powder
175 g/6 oz caster sugar
3 eggs, beaten
1 tbsp milk
40 g/1½ oz chocolate mint sticks, chopped
140 g/5 oz chocolate spread, plus extra to drizzle
chocolate mint sticks, to decorate

>1 Preheat the oven to 180°C/350°F/ Gas Mark 4. Grease and line two 20-cm/8-inch sandwich tins.

>2 Sift the flour, cocoa and baking powder into a bowl and beat in the butter, sugar and eggs, mixing until smooth. Stir in the milk and chocolate mint pieces.

Decorate the cake with
chocolate mint sticks.

>3 Spread the mixture into the tins. Bake in
the preheated oven for 25–30 minutes,
until risen and firm. Cool in the tins for
2 minutes, then turn out onto a wire rack
to cool completely.

>4 Sandwich the cakes together with chocolate
spread. Gently warm a little of the spread
and drizzle it over the top.

pastries

summer fruit tartlets

makes 12 tartlets

ingredients

200 g/7 oz plain flour, plus
  extra for dusting
85 g/3 oz icing sugar, sifted
55 g/2 oz ground almonds
115 g/4 oz butter
1 egg yolk
1 tbsp milk

filling

225 g/8 oz cream cheese
icing sugar, to taste, plus
  extra, sifted, for dusting
350 g/12 oz fresh summer
  berries

> **1** Sift the flour and icing sugar into a bowl. Stir in the almonds. Add the butter, rubbing in until the mixture resembles breadcrumbs. Add the egg yolk and milk and work in until the dough binds together. Wrap in clingfilm and chill for 30 minutes.

> **2** Preheat the oven to 200°C/400°F/ Gas Mark 6. Roll out the dough on a lightly floured surface and use it to line 12 deep tartlet tins. Prick the bases and press a piece of foil into each.

Dust with sifted icing sugar and serve immediately.

>3 Bake in the preheated oven for 10–15 minutes, or until light golden brown. Remove from the oven, remove the foil and place on a wire rack to cool.

>4 Halve the strawberries. For the filling, place the cream cheese and icing sugar in a bowl and mix together. Place a spoonful of filling in each tartlet and arrange the berries on top.

apple danish

makes 12–16 pastries

ingredients

275 g/9¾ oz strong white flour,
  plus extra, sifted, for dusting
175 g/6 oz butter, well chilled,
  plus extra for greasing

½ tsp salt
7 g/¼ oz easy-blend dried
  yeast
2 tbsp caster sugar, plus extra
  for sprinkling

1 egg
1 tsp vanilla extract
6 tbsp lukewarm water
milk, for glazing

filling

2 cooking apples, peeled,
  cored and chopped
grated rind of 1 lemon
3 tbsp sugar

>1 Place the flour in a bowl and rub in 25 g/1 oz of the butter. Set aside. Dust the remaining butter with flour, grate coarsely into a bowl and chill. Stir the salt, yeast and sugar into the flour mixture.

>2 In another bowl, beat the egg with the vanilla extract and water, add to the flour mixture and mix to form a dough. Knead for 10 minutes on a floured surface, then chill for 10 minutes.

>3 Roll out the dough to a 30 x 20-cm/12 x 8-inch rectangle. Mark widthways into thirds and fold. Press the edges with a rolling pin and roll out to the same size as the original rectangle.

>4 Sprinkle the grated butter evenly over the top two-thirds. Fold up the bottom third and fold down the top third. Press the edges, wrap in clingfilm and chill for 30 minutes. Repeat four times, chilling well each time. Chill overnight.

> **5** Mix the filling ingredients together. Preheat the oven to 200°C/400°F/Gas Mark 6. Grease two baking sheets.

> **6** Roll out the dough into a 40-cm/16-inch square and cut into 16 squares. Pile some filling in the centre of each, reserving any juice. Brush the edges of the squares with milk and bring the corners together in the centre.

> **7** Place on the prepared baking sheets and chill for 15 minutes. Brush with the reserved juice and sprinkle with caster sugar.

> **8** Bake in the preheated oven for 10 minutes, reduce the temperature to 180°C/350°F/Gas Mark 4 and bake for a further 10–15 minutes, until browned.

Gently remove from the baking sheets
and serve.

spiced pear & sultana strudel

serves 6

ingredients

85 g/3 oz unsalted butter, melted

3 firm ripe pears, peeled, cored and diced

finely grated rind and juice of ½ lemon

75 g/2¾ oz demerara sugar

1 tsp ground allspice

55 g/2 oz sultanas

55 g/2 oz ground almonds

6 sheets filo pastry (half a 250 g/9 oz pack)

icing sugar, sifted, for dusting

>**1** Preheat the oven to 200°C/400°F/Gas Mark 6 and grease a baking sheet with butter.

>**2** Mix together the pears, lemon rind and juice, sugar, allspice, sultanas and half the almonds.

>**3** Place 2 sheets of filo pastry, slightly overlapping, on a clean tea towel.

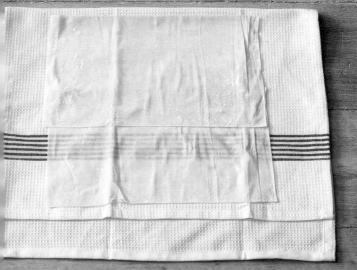

>**4** Brush lightly with melted butter and sprinkle with a third of the almonds. Top with two more sheets, butter and almonds. Repeat once more.

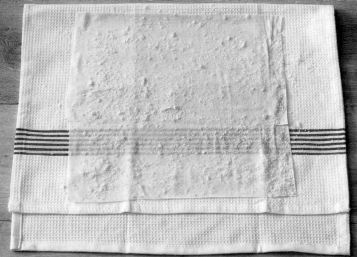

>5 Spread the pear mixture down one long side, to within 2.5 cm/1 inch of the edge.

>6 Roll the pastry over to enclose the filling and roll up, using the tea towel to lift. Tuck the ends under.

>7 Bake in the preheated oven for 20–25 minutes, until golden and crisp.

>8 Lightly dust the strudel with icing sugar.

Serve the strudel warm or cold, cut into thick slices.

chocolate nut strudel

serves 6

ingredients

200 g/7 oz mixed
  chopped nuts
115 g/4 oz plain
  chocolate, chopped
115 g/4 oz milk
  chocolate, chopped
115 g/4 oz white
  chocolate, chopped
200 g/7 oz filo pastry
150 g/5½ oz unsalted
  butter, melted, plus extra
  for greasing
3 tbsp golden syrup
55 g/2 oz icing sugar, sifted,
  for dusting

 >1 Preheat the oven to 190°C/375°F/Gas Mark 5.
Lightly grease a baking sheet. Reserving a
tablespoonful, place the nuts in a bowl and
mix with the chocolate.

>2 Place a sheet of pastry on a clean
tea towel. Brush with butter, drizzle
with some golden syrup and sprinkle
with the nut and chocolate mixture.
Place another sheet on top and
repeat the procedure until you have
used all the nuts and chocolate.

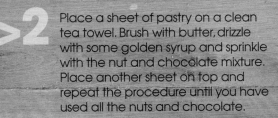

Dust the strudel with icing sugar, slice and serve.

>3 Use the tea towel to carefully roll up the strudel, place on the prepared baking sheet, drizzle with the remaining golden syrup and sprinkle with the reserved nuts.

>4 Bake in the preheated oven for 20–25 minutes. If the nuts start to brown too much, cover the strudel with a sheet of foil.

strawberry éclairs

makes 16–18 éclairs

ingredients

pastry
55 g/2 oz unsalted butter,
  plus extra for greasing
150 ml/5 fl oz water
8 tbsp plain flour, sifted
2 eggs, beaten

filling
200 g/7 oz strawberries
2 tbsp icing sugar
140 g/5 oz mascarpone cheese

>1 Preheat the oven to 220°C/425°F/Gas Mark 7. Grease 2 baking sheets. Heat the butter and water in a pan until boiling.

>2 Remove from the heat, quickly tip in the flour and beat until smooth.

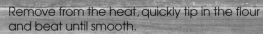

>3 Gradually beat in the eggs with an electric hand mixer, until glossy.

>4 Spoon into a piping bag with a large plain nozzle and pipe up to eighteen 9-cm/3½-inch fingers on the baking sheets.

>5 Bake in the preheated oven for 12–15 minutes, until golden brown. Cut a slit down the side of each éclair to release steam. Bake for a further 2 minutes. Remove from the oven and place on a wire rack to cool.

>6 Purée half the strawberries with the icing sugar.

>7 Finely chop the remaining strawberries and stir into the mascarpone.

>8 Pipe or spoon the mascarpone mixture into the éclairs.

Serve the éclairs with the strawberry purée spooned over. The éclairs are best served within an hour of filling.

119

baklava

serves 16

ingredients

225 g/8 oz walnut halves, finely chopped

225 g/8 oz shelled pistachio nuts, finely chopped

100 g/3½ oz blanched almonds, finely chopped

4 tbsp pine nuts, finely chopped

finely grated rind of 2 large oranges

6 tbsp sesame seeds

1 tbsp sugar

½ tsp ground cinnamon

½ tsp mixed spice

250 g/9 oz butter, melted, plus extra for greasing

23 sheets filo pastry

syrup

450 g/1 lb caster sugar

450 ml/16 fl oz water

5 tbsp honey

3 cloves

> **1** Put the walnuts, pistachios, almonds and pine nuts in a bowl and stir in the orange rind, sesame seeds, sugar, cinnamon and mixed spice.

> **2** Preheat the oven to 160°C/325°F/Gas Mark 3. Grease a 25-cm/10-inch square ovenproof dish, about 5 cm/2 inches deep.

> **3** Stack the pastry sheets. Cut them to the size of the dish, using a ruler.

> **4** Place a sheet of pastry on the base of the dish and brush with melted butter. Top with seven more sheets, brushing with butter between each layer.

>5 Sprinkle with a generous 150 g/5½ oz of the filling. Top with three sheets of pastry, brushing each one with butter. Continue until you have used all the pastry and filling, ending with a top layer of three sheets.

>6 Brush with butter. Cut into 5-cm/2-inch squares. Brush again with butter. Bake in the preheated oven for 1 hour.

>7 Meanwhile, put all the syrup ingredients in a saucepan. Slowly bring to the boil, stirring to dissolve the sugar, then simmer for 15 minutes, without stirring, until a thin syrup forms. Leave to cool.

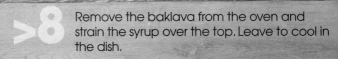

>8 Remove the baklava from the oven and strain the syrup over the top. Leave to cool in the dish.

Cut into squares and serve.

chocolate filo parcels

makes 18 parcels

ingredients

85 g/3 oz ground hazelnuts
1 tbsp finely chopped fresh
  mint
125 ml/4 fl oz soured cream
2 eating apples, peeled and
  grated
55 g/2 oz plain chocolate,
  melted
9 sheets filo pastry, about
  15 cm/6 inches square
55–85 g/2–3 oz butter, melted,
  plus extra for greasing
icing sugar, sifted, for dusting

> **1** Preheat the oven to 190°C/375°F/Gas Mark 5. Grease a baking sheet. Mix the nuts, mint and soured cream in a bowl. Add the apples, stir in the chocolate and mix well.

> **2** Cut each pastry sheet into 4 squares. Brush 1 square with butter, then place a second square on top and brush with butter.

Dust with icing sugar and serve.

>3 Place a tablespoonful of the chocolate mixture in the centre, bring up the corners and twist together. Repeat until all of the pastry and filling has been used.

>4 Place the parcels on the prepared baking sheet and bake in the preheated oven for about 10 minutes, until crisp and golden. Remove from the oven and leave to cool slightly.

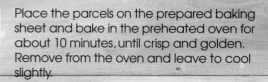

cinnamon swirls

makes 12 swirls

ingredients

25 g/1 oz butter, cut into small
   pieces, plus extra for greasing
225 g/8 oz strong white flour
½ tsp salt

7 g/¼ oz easy-blend dried
   yeast
1 egg, lightly beaten
125 ml/4 fl oz lukewarm milk
2 tbsp maple syrup, for glazing

filling

55 g/2 oz butter, softened
2 tsp ground cinnamon
50 g/1¾ oz soft light brown sugar
50 g/1¾ oz currants

> 1 Grease a baking sheet and a bowl. Sift the flour and salt into a mixing bowl and stir in the yeast.

> 2 Rub in the chopped butter with your fingertips until the mixture resembles breadcrumbs. Add the egg and milk and mix to form a dough.

> 3 Form the dough into a ball, place in the greased bowl, cover and leave to stand in a warm place for about 40 minutes, or until doubled in volume.

> 4 Punch down the dough lightly for 1 minute, then roll out to a rectangle measuring 30 x 23 cm/12 x 9 inches.

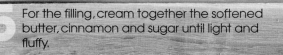

>5 For the filling, cream together the softened butter, cinnamon and sugar until light and fluffy.

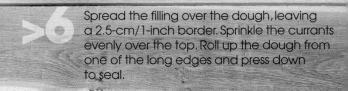

>6 Spread the filling over the dough, leaving a 2.5-cm/1-inch border. Sprinkle the currants evenly over the top. Roll up the dough from one of the long edges and press down to seal.

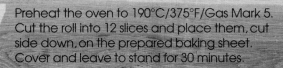

>7 Preheat the oven to 190°C/375°F/Gas Mark 5. Cut the roll into 12 slices and place them, cut side down, on the prepared baking sheet. Cover and leave to stand for 30 minutes.

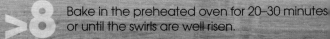

>8 Bake in the preheated oven for 20–30 minutes or until the swirls are well risen.

Brush with maple syrup and leave to
cool slightly before serving.

lemon meringue pie

serves 6–8

ingredients

150 g/5½ oz plain flour, plus
   extra for dusting
85 g/3 oz butter, cut into small
   pieces, plus extra for greasing

35 g/1¼ oz icing sugar, sifted
finely grated rind of ½ lemon
½ egg yolk, beaten
1½ tbsp milk

filling
3 tbsp cornflour
300 ml/10 fl oz water
juice and grated rind of
   2 lemons

175 g/6 oz caster sugar
2 eggs, separated

>1 Sift the flour into a bowl. Rub in the butter with your fingertips until the mixture resembles fine breadcrumbs. Mix in the icing sugar, lemon rind, ½ egg yolk and milk.

>2 Knead briefly on a lightly floured work surface. Wrap in clingfilm and chill in the refrigerator for 30 minutes.

>3 Preheat the oven to 180°C/350°F/Gas Mark 4. Grease a 20-cm/8-inch round tart tin. Roll out the pastry to 5 mm/¼ inch thick, then use it to line the tin.

>4 Prick all over with a fork, line with baking paper and fill with baking beans. Bake in the preheated oven for 15 minutes.

>5 Remove the pastry case from the oven and take out the paper and beans. Reduce the temperature to 150°C/300°F/Gas Mark 2.

>6 For the filling, mix the cornflour with a little water to form a paste. Put the remaining water in a saucepan. Stir the lemon juice and rind into the cornflour paste. Bring to the boil, stirring. Cook for 2 minutes. Cool slightly.

>7 Stir in 5 tablespoons of the caster sugar and the egg yolks, and pour into the pastry case.

>8 Whisk the egg whites in a clean, grease-free bowl until stiff. Gradually whisk in the remaining caster sugar and spread over the pie. Place on a baking sheet and bake for 40 minutes. Remove from the oven and cool.

Serve plain or decorate with whipped
cream and fresh fruit.

cherry & cinnamon tartlets

makes 4 tartlets

ingredients
125 g/4½ oz plain flour, sifted
2 tbsp icing sugar, sifted
½ tsp ground cinnamon
70 g/2½ oz unsalted butter, at
  room temperature
1 egg yolk
2 tbsp cold water

filling
350 g/12 oz cherries, pitted
150 ml/5 fl oz Greek-style yogurt
2 tbsp clear honey
cinnamon and whole cherries,
  to decorate

>1 Preheat the oven to 190°C/375°F/Gas Mark 5. Place the flour, icing sugar, cinnamon and butter in a food processor and process until evenly blended.

>2 Add the egg yolk and water to the mixture, and blend until it just binds to form a soft dough.

Drizzle the tartlets with honey, sprinkle with cinnamon and serve with whole cherries.

>3 Divide the pastry into four and press into 4 x 18-cm/4-inch loose-based tartlet tins, pressing with your knuckles to spread evenly.

>4 Place on a baking sheet and bake the tartlets blind for 12–15 minutes (see page 131), remove from the oven and leave to cool. Stir the cherries into the yogurt and spoon into the cases.

tomato
tarte tatin

serves 4

ingredients

25 g/1 oz butter
1 tbsp caster sugar
500 g/1 lb 2 oz cherry
   tomatoes, halved
1 clove garlic, crushed

2 tsp white wine vinegar
salt and pepper

pastry
250 g/9 oz plain flour, sifted
pinch of salt

140 g/5 oz butter
1 tbsp chopped oregano,
   plus extra to garnish
5–6 tbsp cold water

> 1 Preheat the oven to 200°C/400°F/Gas Mark 6. Melt the butter in a heavy-based pan.

> 2 Add the sugar and stir over a fairly high heat until just turning golden brown.

> 3 Remove from the heat and quickly add the tomatoes, garlic and white wine vinegar, stirring to coat evenly. Season with salt and pepper.

> 4 Tip the tomatoes into a 23-cm/9-inch cake tin, spreading evenly.

5 For the pastry, place the flour, salt, butter and oregano in a food processor and process until the mixture resembles fine breadcrumbs.

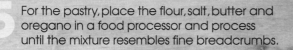 **6** Add just enough water to bind to a soft, but not sticky, dough.

7 Roll out the pastry to a 25-cm/10-inch round and place over the tomatoes, tucking in the edges. Pierce with a fork to let out steam.

8 Bake in the preheated oven for 25–30 minutes, until firm and golden. Rest for 2–3 minutes, then run a knife around the edge and turn out onto a warm serving plate.

Sprinkle the tarte tatin with chopped oregano and serve warm.

broccoli, pancetta & blue cheese galette

serves 4

ingredients

1 sheet ready-rolled puff pastry
(half a pack)
225 g/8 oz small broccoli florets,
halved if necessary
125 g/4½ oz diced pancetta

1 small red onion, sliced
100 g/3½ oz Gorgonzola or
Roquefort cheese, chopped
ground black pepper
toasted pine nuts, to garnish

Preheat the oven to 200°C/400°C/Gas Mark 6. Place the pastry on a baking sheet and lightly score a line all around, cutting only halfway through, to within 1 cm/½ inch of the edge.

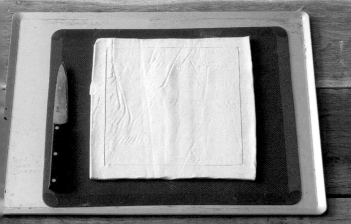

Steam or boil the broccoli for 4–5 minutes, until just tender. Drain.

Fry the pancetta with the onion, stirring, until golden. Stir in the broccoli and season with black pepper.

Spread the filling over the pastry, leaving the border clear.

5 Scatter the pieces of cheese evenly over the top.

6 Bake in the preheated oven for 25–30 minutes, until the pastry is risen and golden.

Sprinkle with toasted pine nuts and serve warm.

asparagus prosciutto wraps

makes 6 wraps

ingredients
225 g/8 oz asparagus,
  trimmed
1 sheet ready-rolled puff
  pastry (half a pack)
2 tbsp pesto
6 thin slices prosciutto
85 g/3 oz grated
  Emmental cheese
milk, for glazing
ground black pepper

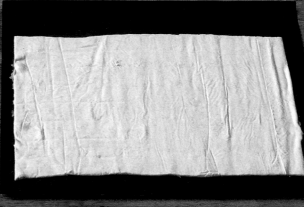

> **1** Preheat the oven to 220°C/425°F/Gas Mark 7. Cook the asparagus in boiling water for 5–6 minutes, until tender. Drain.

> **2** Cut the pastry into 6 squares. Place on a baking sheet and spread 1 tsp pesto on the centre of each.

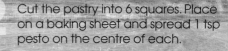

144

Serve the wraps warm or cold, as a lunchtime snack or picnic treat.

3 Divide the asparagus into six bunches and wrap each in a prosciutto slice. Place diagonally on each square and top with grated cheese and pepper.

4 Lift opposite corners over to meet on top, brushing with milk to glaze. Bake in the preheated oven for 15–20 minutes, until golden.

breads

scones

makes 9 scones

ingredients
450 g/1 lb plain flour, plus extra
  for dusting
½ tsp salt
2 tsp baking powder
55 g/2 oz butter
2 tbsp caster sugar
250 ml/9 fl oz milk, plus extra
  for glazing
strawberry jam and clotted
  cream, to serve

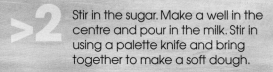

> **>1** Preheat the oven to 220°C/425°F/Gas Mark 7.
> Sift the flour, salt and baking powder into a
> bowl. Rub in the butter using your fingertips
> until the mixture resembles fine breadcrumbs.

> **>2** Stir in the sugar. Make a well in the
> centre and pour in the milk. Stir in
> using a palette knife and bring
> together to make a soft dough.

Serve freshly baked with strawberry jam and clotted cream.

>3 Turn out the dough onto a floured surface and very lightly flatten it until it is 1 cm/½ inch thick. Cut out scones using a 6-cm/2½-inch biscuit cutter and place on a lined baking sheet.

>4 Brush with a little milk and bake in the preheated oven for 10–12 minutes, until golden and well risen. Leave to cool on a wire rack.

plaited poppy seed bread

makes 1 loaf

ingredients

225 g/8 oz strong white flour,
  plus extra for dusting
1 tsp salt
2 tbsp skimmed milk powder
1½ tbsp caster sugar

1 tsp easy-blend dried yeast
175 ml/6 fl oz lukewarm water
2 tbsp vegetable oil, plus extra
  for greasing
5 tbsp poppy seeds

topping

1 egg yolk
1 tbsp milk
1 tbsp caster sugar
2 tbsp poppy seeds

>1 Sift the flour and salt together into a bowl and stir in the milk powder, sugar and yeast. Make a well in the centre, pour in the water and oil and stir until the dough begins to come together.

>2 Add the poppy seeds and knead until fully combined and the dough leaves the side of the bowl. Turn out onto a lightly floured surface and knead well for about 10 minutes, until smooth and elastic.

>3 Brush a bowl with oil. Shape the dough into a ball, put it in the bowl, cover and leave to rise in a warm place for 1 hour, or until doubled in volume.

>4 Oil a baking sheet. Turn out the dough onto a lightly floured surface, knock back and knead for 1–2 minutes. Divide into 3 equal pieces and shape each into a rope 25–30 cm/ 10–12 inches long.

>5 Place the ropes side by side and press together at one end. Plait the dough, pinch the other end together and tuck underneath.

>6 Put the loaf on the prepared baking sheet, cover and leave to rise in a warm place for 30 minutes. Meanwhile, preheat the oven to 200°C/400°F/Gas Mark 6.

>7 For the topping, beat the egg yolk with the milk and sugar. Brush the egg glaze over the top of the loaf and sprinkle with the poppy seeds.

>8 Bake in the preheated oven for 30–35 minutes until golden brown. Transfer to a wire rack and leave to cool.

Serve plain or toasted.

rye bread

makes 1 loaf

ingredients

450 g/1 lb rye flour
225 g/8 oz strong white flour,
  plus extra for dusting

2 tsp salt
2 tsp soft light brown sugar
1½ tsp easy-blend dried yeast
425 ml/15 fl oz lukewarm water

2 tsp vegetable oil, plus extra
  for greasing
1 egg white

>1 Sift the flours and salt together into a bowl. Add the sugar and yeast and stir to mix. Make a well in the centre and pour in the water and oil.

>2 Stir until the dough begins to come together, then knead until it leaves the side of the bowl. Turn out onto a lightly floured surface and knead for 10 minutes, until elastic and smooth.

>3 Brush a bowl with oil. Shape the dough into a ball, put it in the bowl, cover and leave to rise in a warm place for 2 hours, or until doubled in volume.

>4 Oil a baking tray. Turn out the dough onto a lightly floured surface and knock back, then knead for 10 minutes.

>5 Shape the dough into a ball, put it on the prepared baking tray and cover. Leave to rise in a warm place for a further 40 minutes, or until doubled in volume.

>6 Meanwhile, preheat the oven to 190°C/ 375°F/Gas Mark 5. Beat the egg white with 1 tablespoon of water in a bowl.

>7 Bake the loaf in the preheated oven for 20 minutes, then remove from the oven and brush the top with the egg white glaze. Return to the oven and bake for a further 20 minutes.

>8 Brush the top of the loaf with the glaze again and return to the oven for a further 20–30 minutes, until the crust is a rich brown colour. Transfer to a wire rack to cool.

Serve with good quality butter or a
topping of your choice.

irish soda bread

makes 1 loaf

ingredients
butter, melted, for greasing
450 g/1 lb plain flour, plus extra
  for dusting
1 tsp salt
1 tsp bicarbonate of soda
400 ml/14 fl oz buttermilk

>1 Preheat the oven to 220°C/425°F/Gas Mark 7. Lightly grease a baking sheet.

>2 Sift the dry ingredients into a mixing bowl. Make a well in the centre, pour in most of the buttermilk and mix well, using your hands. The dough should be very soft but not too wet. If necessary, add the remaining buttermilk.

Serve in slices with butter and a sweet or savoury topping.

> **3** Turn out the dough onto a floured surface and knead. Shape into a 20-cm/8-inch round.

> **4** Place the bread on the prepared baking sheet, cut a cross in the top and bake in the preheated oven for 25–30 minutes.

crusty white bread

makes 1 loaf

ingredients

1 egg
1 egg yolk
150–200 ml/5–7 fl oz lukewarm
  water

500 g/1 lb 2 oz strong white
  flour, sifted, plus extra for
  dusting
1½ tsp salt
2 tsp sugar

1 tsp easy-blend dried yeast
25 g/1 oz butter, diced
oil, for greasing

>1 Place the egg and egg yolk in a jug and beat lightly to mix. Add enough water to make up to 300 ml/10 fl oz. Stir well.

>2 Place the flour, salt, sugar and yeast in a large bowl. Add the butter and rub it in with your fingertips until the mixture resembles fine breadcrumbs.

>3 Make a well in the centre, add the egg mixture and work to a smooth dough. Turn out onto a lightly floured surface and knead well for about 10 minutes, until smooth.

>4 Brush a bowl with oil. Shape the dough into a ball, place in the bowl, cover and leave to rise in a warm place for 1 hour, or until doubled in volume.

> **5** Preheat the oven to 220°C/425°F/Gas Mark 7. Oil a 900-g/2-lb loaf tin. Turn out the dough onto a lightly floured surface and knead for 1 minute until smooth.

> **6** Shape the dough so it is the same length as the loaf tin and three times the width. Fold the dough in three widthways and place it in the tin with the join underneath.

> **7** Cover and leave in a warm place for 30 minutes, until the dough has risen above the tin.

> **8** Place in the preheated oven and bake for 30 minutes, or until firm and golden brown. Transfer to a wire rack and leave to cool.

Cut into thick slices and serve.

pumpkin & seed twist

makes 1 loaf

ingredients

250 g/9 oz peeled pumpkin, diced

1 tsp fennel seeds

grated rind of 1 lemon

2 tbsp clear honey

500 g/1lb 2 oz strong plain flour

½ tsp salt

6 g sachet easy-blend dried yeast

300 ml/10 fl oz lukewarm water (approx)

oil, for greasing

milk, for glazing

2 tbsp pumpkin and sunflower seeds

1 Steam the pumpkin for 10 minutes or until tender. Drain thoroughly.

>2 Mash the pumpkin and stir in the fennel seeds, lemon rind and honey.

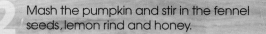

3 Sift the flour and salt into a bowl and stir in the yeast. Add the pumpkin mixture.

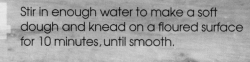

>4 Stir in enough water to make a soft dough and knead on a floured surface for 10 minutes, until smooth.

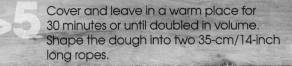

>5 Cover and leave in a warm place for 30 minutes or until doubled in volume. Shape the dough into two 35-cm/14-inch long ropes.

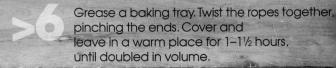

>6 Grease a baking tray. Twist the ropes together, pinching the ends. Cover and leave in a warm place for 1–1½ hours, until doubled in volume.

>7 Preheat the oven to 200°C/400°F/Gas Mark 6. Brush the loaf with milk and sprinkle with pumpkin and sunflower seeds.

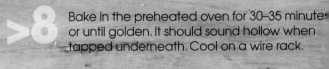

>8 Bake in the preheated oven for 30–35 minutes or until golden. It should sound hollow when tapped underneath. Cool on a wire rack.

Serve the loaf sliced with a hearty winter soup, or for an unusual breakfast.

feta & olive scones

makes 8 scones

ingredients
85 g/3 oz butter, plus extra for
  greasing
400 g/14 oz self-raising flour
¼ tsp salt
40 g/1½ oz pitted black olives,
  chopped
40 g/1½ oz sun-dried tomatoes
  in oil, drained and chopped
85 g/3 oz feta cheese (drained
  weight), crumbled
200 ml/7 fl oz milk, plus extra
  for glazing
ground black pepper

> **1** Preheat the oven to 220°C/425°F/Gas Mark 7.
Grease a baking sheet.

> **2** Sift the flour and salt, and pepper
to taste, into a bowl and rub in the
butter evenly with your fingers.

Serve the scones fresh and warm, with extra butter if needed.

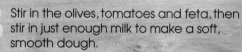 **>3** Stir in the olives, tomatoes and feta, then stir in just enough milk to make a soft, smooth dough.

>4 Roll out on a floured surface to a 3-cm/1¼-inch thick rectangle. Cut into 6-cm/2½-inch squares. Place on the baking sheet, brush with milk and bake for 12–15 minutes, until golden.

stromboli with salami, roasted peppers & cheese

makes 1 loaf

ingredients

500 g/1 lb 2 oz strong white
 flour, sifted
6 g sachet fast-action dried
 yeast
2 tsp sea salt flakes

3 tbsp olive oil, plus extra for
 brushing
350 ml/12 fl oz lukewarm water

filling

85 g/3 oz thinly sliced Italian
 salami
175 g/6 oz mozzarella cheese,
 chopped
25 g/1 oz basil leaves

2 red peppers, roasted,
 peeled, deseeded and sliced
 (or ready-roasted peppers
 from a jar)
freshly ground black pepper

> **1** Mix the flour, yeast and 1½ tsp salt, then stir in the oil with enough water to make a soft dough.

> **2** Knead the dough on a floured surface for about 10 minutes. Cover and leave in a warm place for 1 hour, or until doubled in volume.

> **3** Knead lightly for 2–3 minutes until smooth. Cover and leave for 10 minutes more.

> **4** Roll out the dough to a rectangle about 38 x 25-cm/15 x 10-inch in size, 1 cm/½ inch thick.

Preheat the oven to 200°C/400°F/Gas Mark 6. Spread the salami over the dough and top with the mozzarella, basil and peppers. Season with black pepper.

Grease a baking sheet. Roll the dough up firmly from the long side, pinch the ends and place on the baking sheet. Join underneath. Cover and leave for 10 minutes.

Pierce the roll deeply several times with a skewer.

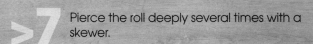

Brush with oil and sprinkle with the remaining salt. Bake in the preheated oven for 30–35 minutes or until firm and golden. Cool on a wire rack.

Serve the bread fresh and warm, cut into thick slices.

173

spring onion & parmesan cornbread

serves 16

ingredients

oil, for greasing
140 g/5 oz fine cornmeal
140 g/5 oz plain flour
4 tsp baking powder

2 tsp celery salt
55 g/2 oz Parmesan cheese, grated
2 eggs, beaten
400 ml/14 fl oz milk

55 g/2 oz butter, melted
1 bunch spring onions, chopped
ground black pepper

>1 Preheat the oven to 190°C/375°F/Gas Mark 5. Grease a 23-cm/9-inch square baking tin.

>2 Sift the cornmeal, flour, baking powder, celery salt and pepper into a bowl and stir in 40 g/1½ oz of the Parmesan.

>3 Beat together the eggs, milk and melted butter.

>4 Add the egg mixture to the dry ingredients and stir well to mix evenly.

>5 Stir in the chopped spring onions and spread the mixture evenly into the tin.

>6 Sprinkle the remaining Parmesan over the mixture. Bake in the preheated oven for 30–35 minutes, or until firm and golden.

Cut the cornbread into squares and serve warm.

pesto & olive soda bread

makes 1 loaf

ingredients

olive oil, for greasing
250 g/9 oz plain flour
250 g/9 oz wholemeal flour
1 tsp bicarbonate of soda
½ tsp salt
3 tbsp pesto
300 ml/½ pint buttermilk,
  (approx)
55 g/2 oz pitted green olives,
  roughly chopped
milk, for glazing

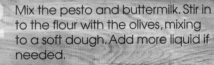

>1 Preheat the oven to 200°C/400°F/Gas Mark 6 and line and grease a baking tray. Sift the flours, bicarbonate of soda and salt into a bowl, adding back any bran from the sieve.

>2 Mix the pesto and buttermilk. Stir in to the flour with the olives, mixing to a soft dough. Add more liquid if needed.

Serve the soda bread on the day of baking.

>3 Shape the dough into a 20-cm/8-inch round and place on the baking tray. Flatten slightly and cut a deep cross with a sharp knife.

>4 Brush with milk and bake in the preheated oven for 30–35 minutes, until golden brown. The loaf should sound hollow when tapped underneath.

chocolate & saffron brioches

makes 12 brioches

ingredients

pinch of saffron strands
3 tbsp boiling water
55 g/2 oz butter, melted
250 g/9 oz strong plain flour

pinch of salt
1 tbsp caster sugar
6 g sachet easy-blend dried
  yeast
2 eggs, beaten

6 squares plain dark chocolate,
  halved (30 g/1 oz total)
milk, for glazing

>1 Add the saffron to the boiling water and leave to cool completely.

>2 Lightly brush 12 individual brioche tins or fluted bun tins with butter.

>3 Sift the flour, salt and sugar and stir in the yeast. Add the saffron, liquid, eggs and remaining butter to make a soft dough.

>4 Knead until smooth, then cover and leave in a warm place for 1–1½ hours, or until doubled in volume.

>5 Knead briefly then shape three-quarters of the dough into 12 balls. Place in the tins and press a piece of chocolate firmly into each.

>6 Shape the remaining dough into 12 small balls with a pointed end. Brush with milk and press the balls in each bun, sealing well.

>7 Cover with oiled clingfilm and leave in a warm place for 1½ hours, or until doubled in volume.

>8 Preheat the oven to 200°C/400°F/Gas Mark 6. Brush with milk and bake in the preheated oven for 12–15 minutes, until firm and golden.

Turn out the brioches and serve warm.

fresh croissants

makes 6 croissants

ingredients

500 g/1 lb 2 oz strong white
  flour, sifted, plus extra
  for dusting
40 g/1½ oz caster sugar

1 tsp salt
2 tsp easy-blend dried yeast
300 ml/10 fl oz lukewarm milk
300 g/10½ oz butter, softened,
  plus extra for greasing

1 egg, lightly beaten with
1 tbsp milk, for glazing

> 1 Preheat the oven to 200°C/400°F/ Gas Mark 6. Mix the dry ingredients in a large bowl, make a well in the centre and add the milk. Mix to a soft dough, adding more milk if too dry.

> 2 Knead on a lightly floured work surface for 5–10 minutes, or until smooth and elastic. Place in a large greased bowl, cover and leave in a warm place until doubled in volume.

> 3 Meanwhile, place the butter between two sheets of baking paper and flatten with a rolling pin to form a 5-mm/¼-inch thick rectangle. Set aside in the refrigerator until required.

> 4 Knead the dough for 1 minute. Remove the butter from the refrigerator. Roll out the dough on a well-floured work surface to 45 x 15 cm/ 18 x 6 inches.

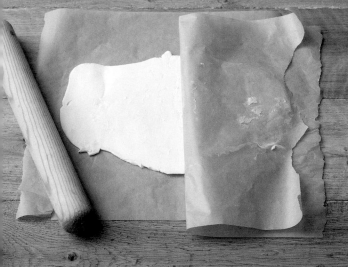

>5 Place the butter in the centre of the dough, folding up the sides and squeezing the edges together gently. With the short end of the dough towards you, fold the top third down and the bottom third up.

>6 Give the dough a quarter turn, roll out as big as the original rectangle and fold again. If the butter feels soft, wrap the dough in clingfilm and chill. Repeat the rolling process twice more.

>7 Cut the dough in half and roll out each half into a 5-mm/¼-inch thick rectangle. Use a cardboard triangular template, base 18 cm/7 inches and sides 20 cm/8 inches, to cut out the croissants.

>8 Brush the triangles with the glaze. Roll into croissant shapes, tucking the point underneath. Brush again with the glaze. Place on a baking sheet and leave to double in volume. Bake in the preheated oven for 15–20 minutes, until golden brown.

Serve with a sweet or savoury filling.

cinnamon spiced orange beignets

makes 8 beignets

ingredients
250 g/9 oz plain flour
1 tsp easy-blend dried yeast
1½ tbsp caster sugar
125 ml/4 fl oz lukewarm milk
1 egg, beaten
finely grated rind of 1 small
   orange
1 tsp orange flower water
40 g/1½ oz butter, melted
sunflower oil, for deep frying
cinnamon sugar, for dusting
orange slices or segments,
   to serve

>**1** Sift the flour into a bowl and stir in the yeast and sugar.

>**2** Add the milk, egg, orange rind, flower water and butter and mix to a soft dough, kneading until smooth.

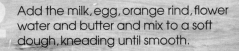

Sprinkle with cinnamon sugar and serve hot with orange slices or segments.

>3 Cover and leave in a warm place until doubled in volume. Roll out on a lightly floured surface to 1 cm/½ inch in thickness, and cut into eight 7.5-cm/3-inch squares.

>4 Heat the oil to 180°C/350°F. Fry the beignets in batches until golden brown. Remove with a slotted spoon and drain on kitchen paper.